OBOE

THREE OLD FRENCH

Freely transcribed by
JANET CRAXTON and
ALAN RICHARDSON

IS

1. L'AGRÉABLE

© Copyright 1962, 1989 Chester Music Ltd.,
8/9 Frith Street, London. W1V 5TZ

2. LA PROVENÇALE

Freely transcribed by
JANET CRAXTON and
ALAN RICHARDSON

MARIN MARAIS
(1656-1728)

Allegretto vivo

3. LE BASQUE

Freely transcribed by
JANET CRAXTON and
ALAN RICHARDSON

MARIN MARAIS
(1656-1728)

Printed by Caligraving Limited, Thetford, Norfolk, England

THREE OLD FRENCH DANCES

Freely transcribed by
JANET CRAXTON and
ALAN RICHARDSON

MARIN MARAIS
(1656 - 1728)

1. L'AGRÉABLE

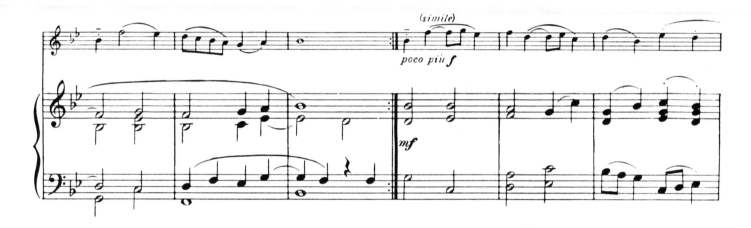

2. LA PROVENÇALE

Freely transcribed by
JANET CRAXTON and
ALAN RICHARDSON

MARIN MARAIS
(1656-1728)

3. LE BASQUE

Freely transcribed by
JANET CRAXTON and
ALAN RICHARDSON

MARIN MARAIS
(1656-1728)